The Seeds We Sow

Alexis Jaimes

The Seeds We Sow

ISBN: 978-1-966337-36-2
First Edition, 2026

Printed in the United States of America

Edited by: Hannah Astrid Noble
Cover Design by: Dulce (dulcenopronto)
Layout Design by: Hannah Astrid Noble

Para
Todas las mujeres que sufren cada día
que siempre abrazan la esperanza
que luchan a su manera contra la circunstancias
mujeres como mi madre

For
My partner
My best friend
My reason
Hannah, I love you
Life is impossible without someone like you

For
The tongue-tied
The abused
The marginalized
The ones who are too tough on themselves
The ones questioning their existence
Please stay

For
a better future
where ICE is abolished
where Palestine is free
where everyone is free

PRAISE FOR THE SEEDS WE SOW

"Alexis Jaimes's *The Seeds We Sow* is a stunning meditation on family, generational trauma, mental illness, poverty, culture, faith, and social justice. Continuing and expanding on the themes of his chapbook, *Corazón Coalesced*, he asks us to consider: how much suffering is too much? When do we decide to speak up? Stand up? Carve out a new home for ourselves? As we span his childhood and family history to the present day, he highlights the cost of bottling up our pain, as well as the vastness that's opened up when we free ourselves of judgment and fear. Visually speaking, my favorite poems are those that are shaped into the subject of the poem: 'On Our Watch' as a weapon, 'Winds of change' as a passing breeze, 'I want to' as a record player. Longing, urgent, and passionate, this is a debut collection not to be missed."

— Sofía Aguilar, author of *amor.* and *STREAMING SERVICE: the series finale*

"Alexis Jaimes' words take you on a trip through his heart to his soul and ultimately through your heart and your soul. The passion in his love poems reminds you that there is a reason to live, and that reason is to love, despite the pain and unfairness of the thing we call love. His anger and frustration come out raw and pure, to hit you in the face with the reality of a punch to wake you up from apathy. But it is in his poems dedicated to his family where you find the tenderness of his soul. He reminds us of what it means to feel at home, with all its imperfections and difficulties, but also love and honesty as he writes 'these people/round a square table/the main attraction plays along/boasting he never missed them too much/He did.' To immerse oneself in Alexis Jaimes' words is to take a trip through this experience we call life, and after all, that is what one searches for in poetry."

—Jesus Cortez, author of *whispering to god and the city*

"*The Seeds We Sow* teaches us, that by reclaiming our stories, we can dismantle what has sought to demonize us. We gain the ability to not only liberate our mind but in turn extend grace to the body. We can pass down the language to those who came before us and can reclaim the full self, despite its complexity. Jaimes explores grief, loss, and breaks the narrative both in form and subject to increase access to conversations we previously lacked the language to hold. A bold series of poetry that fights for a better tomorrow."

— Lizeth De La Luz, Poet

"Alexis' collection is beautifully written through each word and stanza. Two of my favorite poems are 'you're free' and 'SIRENS' due to the powerful message and strategic structure. Excited for readers to read this amazing collection."

— Celeste Alyssa Gomez, author & founder of La Poeta Publications

"*The Seeds We Sow* by Alexis Jaimes is a collection of beautifully heartbreaking poems, full of stories on the pains, aches, and worthwhile parts of living in this world. Jaimes captures each of his experiences into stanzas of thoughtful language, allowing readers to understand life through his eyes. Throughout this book, we learn about what it means to love, to survive, to be angry, to fight back, to escape, and to dream; it is an unapologetic reminder that 'our existence is an act of resistance.'"

— samantha "sammy" herrera, author of *how to stay afloat: the art of drowning*

"What happens when you carefully peel the prickly skin of confession and survival but an open palmed manifestation like *The Seeds We Sow*. Alexis Jaimes demonstrates all that must be broken, torn and unwrapped in order to get to the sweet nectar of life. As shown in poems like 'How to Survive a Heat Wave in Santa Ana' and 'Two-Legged Rat/Rata de dos patas,' the author's words go down like an exquisite fermented drink. Forthright and tender, Jaimes offers a path forward from the ruins of oppression with words like 'let this night lower its knives/let this match light the new day/let this brick guide my throw/let us/keep us safe.'"

— Anatalia Vallez, author of *The Most Spectacular Mistake*

"*The Seeds We Sow* is a fertile field of stories of survival, inheritance, and family planted with love and necessity. In this debut poetry collection, Jaimes does not mince his words; with sharp writing made to rupture, he takes a blade to the star-spangled banner and carves out enough space for the hopes of immigrants to truly become the American dream. Jaimes' mastery of imagery is indelible and poignantly paints the gripping, Chicano coming-of-age tale of a proud son of immigrants. This collection is raw and loud; you can hear the wail of sirens, the blaring brass of banda, the heavy breaths, and the utter silence in crushing moments. *The Seeds We Sow* proves that living is an act of defiance in a world that doesn't want us and shows that joy, love, language and memory become the most vital forms of resistance."

— Peter Lechuga, author of *Myth Opportunities*

"In *The Seeds We Sow*, Alexis Jaimes does exactly what the title promises: he plants seeds that will continue to grow and bloom long after you've read its final pages. These poems carry a rare combination of strength and tenderness, proving the two can exist simultaneously and that one does not weaken the other. It is here that Jaimes offers his own kind of rebellion—his refusal to surrender his artistry and become like the world that surrounds him. One of the book's most powerful lines appears in the poem 'I Was Told': I will not be domesticated by shame because I am proud, I am what my ancestors made me." And man—the ancestors must be proud!"

— Oscar Velazquez, Poet

CONTENTS

Mango

Sabes quererme | You know how to love me

Sábila

Sacando espinas | Extracting the spines

Nopal

Suave como espinas
Soft like spines

Go

Mom took the keys & left her purse behind.
She grabbed my arm & cocked those lethal words:
"I'm taking him with me." The cops arrived
& found us holding hands on a street curb.
Dad wore a golden cross around his neck.
He always skipped mass, & that was a sin.
The Sunday class he forced me to attend
has taught me that I should be less like him.
The house with Christmas lights in mid-July
was mine. The front was where I held Mom's hands
& wished for them to get along that night.
I said I did; I didn't understand.
  I ran away once I found out I could.
  This time I'll leave like Mom promised we would.

somniphobia

most nights / my head swells with questions that evolve / from curiosity / to wonder / to mental illness / to looking out my window at 3:31 A.M. / recognizing that the neighbor's blue Corolla isn't parked in the driveway / which is too bad because it's street sweeping day / & I hope they're bad people / because good people don't deserve bad things / good people like you / who distort my dreams into worries / I think of you / present & future / whether you'll get what you deserve / if it's fair / that the most beautiful people I know think they're hideous / that they slice their flesh / hoping to feel something different / that I'm still breathing while others aren't / I'll blame you / as I hear the hopeless at 4:07 A.M. / who plow the silence with screams / shattering the serenity / reminding me that I'm only deaf in the left ear / meaning I can still hear / death approaching / but there's still so much life here

voicemail

it ended

with the sound of pills clattering like cold teeth
with the sound of breaths caught & released

with the sound of

I never got to say
    how I wanted to bleach their hair again
    & stain another shirt neon-something
    while Paramore echoes the bathroom walls

    that I attended Mr. Lawhon's class just to sit next to her
    that it was her fault I started & why I put it down
    that she taught me to bend enough before I break

    or that I am sorry becaused I promised to always answer

I've contemplated how I would go
but I'll leave a message if I ever do
probably a voicemail
as an apology for calling

or never doing so in the first place

Things I did because I could as soon as I turned 18:

- moved five hundred miles away
- dyed my hair blue
- then green
- rinse and repeat
- got a lip ring
- ditched work study
- spent FAFSA on weed
- and munchies
- dreamed big
- wished for friends
- had friends move in
- fed random neighborhood cats with friends
- watched friends drop out
- helped them move out
- best friend still living with me so it's okay
- searched craigslist for roommates
- met lesbian roommates
- gave them the keys and skipped signing the lease
- drank the tea Gabby made
- heard them make each other moan at night
- missed best friend as she visited boyfriend on weekends
- called the police when Tanya gave Gabby a black eye
- saw them return from the police station holding each other
- acted as if they weren't ignoring me
- heard them moan again at midnight
- pretended they weren't arguing the next morning
- regretted not having them sign the lease
- talked to them about overdue rent
- scoffed at them when they asked for the bigger bedroom
- told them we had an agreement
- smoked to sleep
- smoked to wake
- smoked to feel less alone
- set so much fire to my body I began coughing up ashes
- woke up daily to lava bubbling my insides
- evicted lesbian couple from Craigslist who didn't sign the lease
- went to visit back home
- never returned

finding freedom from your abusers is not cowardness

don't worry
i'll scrub the walls clean of my presence
you'll never know i was here
just like you always wanted
here's a favor for you
& myself
i'll forget because that's how i cope
you'll drink because that's how you do

i never thought i'd leave this house
but it hasn't been a home for a while
it'll be better this way
won't it?

& no, it isn't running way
this is i can't stand you
this is escape
finding freedom from your abusers is not cowardness

you wouldn't understand
it's not fútbol
not a '97 accord
not something that could be fixed with your hands—only broken—
nights like these leave nothing worth having behind

but you're still part of me
& i hate that
i despise whatever part of me came from you—unwanted gift—
that's what i was

no
not anymore
it's about what i am now

i am your curse
i will haunt you
i will traumatize your nights reminding you why you don't deserve sleep
i will live & that's my greatest revenge
my joy will strangle all of you i have left with a smile

not you

this is about fire
not you

it's about
how insatiable it is
how it feasts on all flesh with inverted fangs
claiming its territory with ashes
it's like the hickeys you called vampire kisses
that acted as stakes planted on my neck
that held arteries as hostages
& seared unloved skin

but
this is about fire

& about
how deceitful it is
how it draws everyone in like a moth
knowing moths are stupid
promising the flames won't hurt
& if it scalds
it's not on purpose

so
when you singed me
i still stayed
i swallowed your lies
even though it tasted like burnt skin

but
this is not about you

it's about fire
about how beautiful it is
about how it seduces pupils with exotic dance
about how it tries its best to crackle songs
about how the hues remind me of your cheeks
when we spent school nights lying on wet sand

daring each other to make the first move

this is not about you
or how your hunger makes my stomach turn
or that your mane resembles the subject of this poem

it's about fire
& how it is like you

Denial

when he turned to me
he cleared his throat & gave a look that pleaded for help

that's how I knew it would be serious
but teenage boys aren't supposed to be serious

so I don't act like it is
but I do act annoyed & ask what he wants

his chest rises
draws in the air that mixed with the bus exhaust to whisper

I am bi

my eyes pull away like I saw something I shouldn't have
like I heard something I shouldn't have

like I didn't deserve to know this
or maybe I didn't want to

because even though we've known each other since kinder
I haven't grown much kinder

this isn't a time to kid around
must act cool

I know

is not what you tell someone who finds something reassuring in you someone who can sing falsetto, smile like an angel, & fall from heaven for loving blasphemously

I am unprepared, immature, & cruel

then he adds

I am serious

our eyes meet
mine look away

Me too

I subtract
the amber in his eyes dim as he asks not to tell anyone anyway

I don't & act like I didn't hear a thing
he is still straight

we are still good friends
& I'm the only one in denial

It takes effort to make it look effortless

they romanticized your loneliness not knowing they mistook it
for choice
for purpose

as if being depressed to the point of self-destruction was beautiful
something to envy
to long for
& it is not
it is crippling

& it is scheduling appointments with the school
psychologist online because the thought of
using a phone other than to feed your
withdrawal from others tightens its grip
around your throat

& as you wheeze for air
your sight blurs
your senses dull to a numbness
painful to the touch

like ice searing the fingertips
like voices saying you're better than this
like yours agreeing to it

instances like these are too common
what's worse is they're unseen

except for the times you win
the small victories they call normal
& these miracles that are the foundation of your
very
function
remain unnoticed

again

whenever it's cold I feel you too
the distance between us & the time back then shortens
the horizons change but the atmosphere smells familiar
my joints ache
spine shrivels
an exhale spreads out against a bruised skyline

it feels like home away from home again
the numbness begins to wear off

I am tender again
I am vulnerable to those feelings I thought were extinct ages ago
trapped in slumber running down untouched cheeks

it smells like menthol cigarettes again
my head grows lighter
only I don't hesitate to inhale the secondhand
I try to keep it in
I don't want any trace of you to leave
but
I cough like I always did

my eyes are red again
surrounded in saltwater
I rub the sentiment off onto a rolled fist
I see shards of light looking like pieces of broken glass
because nothing ever remains intact
not even this

it feels like last time
my words loiter in the space between us
heavy with desperation sinking into oblivion
like we always did

then
you're gone
again

Where it should be

When I get asked why I left in the first place
I return the favor with another question
a boomerang tossed by accident
nevertheless slices the air
& the question rotates so fast it blurs
to eyes searing with tears
—a record skipping where the voice should be—
the notes are stuck in a crevice where the groove should be
& she is where I should be

I was told things don't always turn out the way you want
such words wrap softly
tighter until the blur becomes clearer
enough that the question
burning with stomach acid
claws out of my throat:

Have you ever felt desperate enough to try anything to alleviate your pain?

Fodder for the Fire & Fathers

you'll find me where the skies aren't blue
forever morose like the lilies tilting toward tomorrow

& the air
composed of glows from sparks lighting the oblivion ablaze

as I caress something so unreal it'll feel like it is
the tangible
gargles
& beats—
                swaying
                        in
                  the
                      heat

as I remain tangled in its embrace

I won't leave

a promise so profound
that nails   dig   into fists
holding onto nothing but blood
& desperation

I waiver knowing this was always a lie
trembling
knowing I'd never again
        dance with the trees in the whirlwind swirling us
        hear the songs rivers play when they overwhelm entire
                landscapes
        look up to constellations to guide me during the long
                nights

Nor will tears taste any sweeter than it does right now

Watch
as it evaporates to where I will meet it, too

No sign of forced entry

Summer break ends
with my parents driving me 400
miles to a door stamped 292.

We arrive before the sun did.

My parents rest in my room while
I went to meet her.

I sit across to face her sideways
spine.

She sleeps in an oversized t-shirt
that melts onto the living room
floor.

Her red blanket resembles a pool
of blood with the ripples sprawling
out.

I inspect her with caffeine eyes
like a dog searching for a scent—a
warning.

Moonlight pierces the glass sliding
door guiding me through the
waves of her hair & scattered
belongings:
A copy of *The Count of Monte Cristo*,
a comb with missing teeth, & her
backpack bursting at the seams
spewing underwear.

I whisper.

She whispers back.

I ask if she wants to celebrate.

Celebrate what?
You. Welcome.
Celebrate how?

We tiptoe outside to sit in
our patio,
scraping open the plastic
chairs.

I toss her a plastic container
& my pipe
explaining that new people
break the bud.

We trade stories of our
suicide attempts like little
kids do with Pokémon cards.
She fits in better than her
shirt does.

She asks what I did during
the summer.

Go home. Visit for a while, I
guess. We all do.

I nod to the other
roommates.

She would be evicted a few
months later & keep the key
as a souvenir.

When I return next summer
break, it shouldn't be a
surprise why the PlayStation
is missing or where the futon
went or why there was no
sign of forced entry.

jumped

Brother comes home with a black eye
that is welcomed by the shriek from Amá that pierces the paper-
thin walls

Her big brown eyes
        overpoured hope into a vessel never taught to handle it
        like one of papi's shot glasses he demanded to conceal a
                                                    lifetime of pain
now slit shut by the wrinkles she gathered over the years
leaving tears to overcome fleshy levees   still doing so

This is the asthma attack he had at 14 all over again
only, this time there are no uniformed men pressing down his chest
absent are the cacophony
        of his wheezing gasping for air
        grunts from effort cracking open the lungs
        sirens drowning the scene in a red sea

Yet my eyes are still shut
viewing is optional
& if I can't see it
it doesn't exist

Yes, it is childish
but I am a child who didn't ask for this
I am too young
to witness

What a lifetime of gasping next to a freeway does to the organs
or
how a zip code determines your health & foresees your poverty
or
machismo with a moustache for a father
or
the consequences of believing in SkyPapi over health professionals
or
how expensive it is to ride a deafening vehicle to the hospital
or

the effects of a systemic power beyond my control like
the difficulties of raising a baby in a world where they call him
anchor

& him
believing that what it takes to feel belonging isn't the blood shared
in the veins
but the broken vessels around the eyes
to show
you share trauma with others who hurt others to feel less alone

still, I am not too young to experience it

A Poem Against Banda

I tell my friends I hate banda
whatever that means
that it's proud & thunderous not triumphant but like a cuete weeks
before the fourth
wanting to be seen & heard
deemed illegal because it's dangerous
because its shine can spread
blinding those who dare peek

it hurts
that the sound so synonymous with who I'm viewed as
who I am
is a cacophony
vignettes into a child of immigrants
of an alcoholic father & an enabling mother
who met in a Sizzler as dishwasher & cook
the American dream born out of such a thing

the brass signals an apocalypse—a dissolution of a
family—
it pummels my heart
it's not music it is manipulation
it is a reminder of what a relationship lacks
it is school nights peeking out the window to see my role
model
showing me what not to do
those bloodshot eyes weren't his but maybe they were
something kept hidden for nearly a lifetime
or exposed the entire time

I am plucked to then
it rams into my ears
from the Yukon that never ran
& the yellow pickup that did
the one that always picked me up from school
with the siren that played when in reverse
with "familia" in cursive on the dash cover from the
swap meet

now *I* am in reverse
to
times papi spent entire nights face down
toilet bowls or utility buckets

to
when he'd hand over a McDouble to the unhoused man lying in
front of the liquor store

to
a bong thrown at him by his eldest son

to
his wife pleading for him to stop texting someone else not her

to
him leaving the gate open
& him leaving me wondering where the dog went, again
then another again
& again

I ponder whether I hate banda because he loved it so much
but I tell my friends I don't because it's kind of just too loud

If I took papi to the Palm Reader

The Palm Reader would see:

Boils that swell on hands I swear were once soft
now callous & reach for something behind me
hardened into fists
shaped into hammers
needing to be pried open finger by finger unraveling

palms
that crawled their way beneath a border
that fed the flames for minimum wage
that found my mother doing the same
that held hope tighter than Catholic faith
that signed a mortgage with Green Card fingers
that caressed a bundle of me
that worked under the table & over the roof
that spanked me for breaking the garage door window
that wielded a belt when spanking wasn't enough
that gripped glass bottles searching escape
that wondered why his father hung himself
& if he should do the same

that led to brown arms—a garden planted with welts—
with burns shaped like stripes & scabs like stars

The Palm Reader would see:
the true American Dream

Mago

silence superseded the oxygen machine
peace veiled the frame
& stillness
    no movement
    no inhale
    no one there but what once was

what once was
    no longer struggling to breathe
    no more diapers in size small because she shrunk so much
    no more morphine reverting her to a profound fog

none of that was anymore

what is now
    waiting for the ambulance to take her
    regret for more than could ever be

it's gentle outside & in
the groceries she picked are still there
she would have loved to use them

a band of young mariachi across the street rehearse
but it's the Santa Ana parrots flying free that sang the sweetest song

& then they took her away just like that

Guayaba

Dulce como amarga

As sweet as it is bitter

4th Street & Grand Avenue

On the corner of la cuatro & Grand,
where sex workers sought employment,
stood la Iglesia de Nuestra Señora de Guadalupe.
A porcelain Mary, taller & paler than the real one,
endured outside
protected by metal bars & a moat of cacti.

Down la cuatro,
the trees were decorated in graffiti.
I took this street to misa
where they sold bibles
& bottles of holy salt water
that abuelas bought with rattling copper.

South of Grand was where I fell for a believer—
a Gemini who sipped ginseng tea
& wore a plastic rosary.
For Christmas, I gave her a stolen ring
made of blue cubic zirconia laid into a cross.

She said I was a Virgo & we were too different.

Lavanderia

There she is
pulling clothes out & pushing piles into machines
with the help of little brother
or maybe son
or maybe cousin
or maybe kind stranger

here, we are all familia

She is a chemist, a doctor, a witch in one generation & a mother
of a god in the previous
She is an apothecary, an apprentice because she still needs help
from an elder—guidance
She feeds purple, green, blue potions into metal cubes turning
dirty laundry to this week's
clothing

Man in a blue hat carries around an empty mayo jar rattling with
coins & crumpled dollars
His sign reads
Jesus se murió el pasado domingo
Today we celebrate by cleaning
los domingos are about washing away last week's sins
At least that's what it was when I used to go to church
It remains for others though

The blue hat bobs around in a quiet voice & loud gestures
slapping two palms together & slicing the air was a display of
appreciation

No one truly knows if it's a scam
Jesus might be real
or the photo of him on the jar was downloaded from Google
with the watermarks & borders intact
or it could be true because so many die young around these parts

What’s one more they say—
one too many

The magic woman pulls & pushes burdens into the drying machine
the 50-cent one because it fits all the clothes
The other elders train the younger ones
They continue the tradition & teach—as other generations have—
that this struggle is necessary
& they say:
this pain will make you a kinder person
because then you will understand what it means to work hard
& others will make fun of you for that
& that will make you hurt
& that hurt—that metallic taste you feel in your chest—is what will make you a kinder person
don’t let the mercy be burnt out of you
like a candle left at church
because we are all magic
& we know how to make potions
& use them to turn dirt into clean

How to Survive a Heat Wave in Santa Ana

Reach for the nearest limb
& grip it tenderly

twist
until the stem gives in

scrape the surface with your fingerprints

open wide with canines in sight

plunge into the flesh
with the full ferocity of the mandible

    further
        further
            further

dig past the crust to the core

savor the roots
        the soil
            the carcass of life

Then
reach for the nearest limb again

gentrifying times (bleaching the brown)

It is called progress
but it's really
a father bringing his son
to an unfamiliar barbershop

where the man looks around to
what was his once

where white tile stands on salted soil that used to be
home of orange groves
built by brown hope

where the abandoned strands kiss
something so posh
the new owner—
the son,
the one who knows it all—
doesn't wonder if his father is still here

Amtrak moans into the midnight

A whale song of progress echoes down alleys & spray-painted trees
rumbling through disrupted life
waking the awaken
            spiders in the sinks
            roaches underneath
            cats hunting the mice
                & the people who set poison for them all

Headlights blur in & out of focus
leaving traces of ruby smoldering
underneath the smog that steadily rises
sprawling into the shadows
as rubber scrapes onto the asphalt
leaving scars that read *I was here*

A howl full of hurt is swallowed by the oblivion
leaving only reverberations down paper-thin walls
leaving only
the awaken—
            spiders
            roaches
            cats
                & the people who set poison for them all

Next

pack it all up
we're on to the next place
the last one was burned down
for money

what else?

tradition—
it's how it's always been
& how it's always going to be
it's all we know but

what do we know?

at this new place
where the birds come to pray
standing on elms
looking down

are they next or us?

we're just like a disease
parasites onto ourselves
will the leaves ever

reach the ground again?

& we'll still say
we're in love with it all
then wonder what we can do
we stand in shock
but not enough to stop
the leaves have teeth
shaped like saws
their veins match ours
yet we say we're not related at all

they feel, right?

they inhale hurt
they wail through arsons
their roots deeper than ours won't allow them to run

but we will
to the next one
& the next one

and the next one, right?

how hummingbirds became metal

If anyone denies evolution
point to the heavens

ask them
to explain
how hummingbirds became metal

then oh, my god!
evolving so fast they spout a spotlight
beaming onto the sinners—the guilty until proven innocent

oh, my god!
evolving so fast they shrink, condensing into a casing,
flapping faster than before
a lead bill piercing accused skin

ask them
to explain
how keyboards learned to crawl

then oh, my god!
evolving so fast their tails dropped off
picking up tongues, propagating virtual mirages

oh, my god!
evolving so fast they're warping reality
tangling the mass of loose ends
into a squirming rat king

&

ask them
to explain
how stars solidified into satellites

oh, god!
evolving so fast they dive through the atmosphere
sprouting flames on solar panels

oh, god!
the cosmos is colliding with its creators
smoothing the creases of humanity off the crust
the stars are shooting as we raise our hands

    oh, god!
        oh, god!
            oh, go-!

Canary

What's your canary?
What's your last straw?
When do you know enough is enough?

The moment a child draws their last gasp?
The second swastikas return as a red cap?

The plumes will plunge &
the vertebrae will invert

only
& only
when it's already too late

Last shift

On my last shift at Home Depot, I am asked why I'm leaving and
I say, freshly dropped out of college,
            it's time to move on.

A 21 year old year saying this means nothing. Marco from the
plumbing department stops by, telling me
            Young man, go get that piece of paper.

He continues, *If I had one, life would be different.* He is a trained
plumber with decades of experience, telling me to
            dive into debt for a degree.

I prepare to tell him that I'll probably end up behind a desk
suffocated in decks of documents snarled at by someone who never
            fed off food stamps.

That is until our eyes exchange and the exhaustion beneath his
becomes apparent as if the shade of a sundial never moved forward
            and rested in place.

The knee brace below the hem of his cargo shorts stretched in
Velcro tears, holding the trembling joints as tremors
            rocked the foundation of his body.

It holds him long enough to endure for a future knee replacement.
His ligaments are wise enough to tell me I should get that paper,
            so I'll follow that advice.

On Our Watch

When
did poo-tee-weet turn to
police sirens piercing the peace?

When
did feathers floating to the earth become
replaced with brown bodies?

When
did butterflies devolve to bullets
that now riddle the chests of unarmed children?

When
did candles for the virgen succumb to the number of candles
lit for the mijos they took?

When
now the only rains come
from tears of madres

bottled at the source
for media consumption

depicted as
suspect not son

patient to shot
from justice

to just us

to unjust

Two-Legged Rat / Rata de dos patas

After, Paquita la del Barrio & Paris Paloma & Fall Out Boy

maldito
            patriarcado
                                    podrido
telling mis amigas
                          primas
                                         familia
what to wear on a girl's night to Mission Bar in downtown
as they are

hit up
hunted down
by some broccoli-headed boys
flaunting apestoso-ass cologne
parading egos like a crown
with gestures
mirroring jesters

mira,
pinches ratas de dos patas,
no te odio
te compadezco

has anyone told you
the shiny T on your chest
is not an accessory
for someone so unholy?

mistaking chivalry for misogyny
can't spell
misogyny
with no magic to begin with

you
who bitches about *getting bitches*
            calling them *females*
            calling them *hoes*
            calling them your property to own

to use
to discard
to abuse

I am speaking to you, inútil
who thinks getting political means
calling for repealing the 19th
claiming
Your body,
my choice
is just a joke

ordering your partner to feed you
when you just ate
so, wipe the shit off your lips
those billionaires really appreciate it

wondering why *females* are appalled
at you justifying the enslavement of all
women
of color
of pride
of attitude
of the ability to deny
of the will to resist
of the desire to live

are you listening, inútil?

Cuánto daño nos has hecho
with your thoughts
or there lack of

When the blood releases from the clutches of your cock
does the post-nut clarity allow you to see?

understand that fear
is not a sign of affection
it's not an act of love if you have to make her
it's not bursting the capillaries in her eyes

          with your lack of consent
          with your command for more children
          with your hands around her throat

you
want a maid to pick up after
you
mistake a partner with a mother
grow   the   fuck   up

Cuánto daño nos has hecho

realize
you are why
women have to remember:
you are what you love
not who claims to love you

Cuánto daño nos has hecho

you
are why my mother stayed
in a loveless, abusive relationship
killing her & her children
all in the name of appeasing
a man who cheats, steals, demands
a man who never went to church but claims
God made us in his image
that he
is a He
that there are no mistakes
& this is meant to be

Cuánto daño nos has hecho

offer scars & stretchmarks, Rib
you are part of Adam & you owe him
but they don't tell you about Lilith
who left Eden
& how she called Adam
una rata de dos patas

te odio, inútil
so, watch your back
for those whose trunks carry baseball bats

you
aren't the only one capable of hurting
ensure las brujas burn entirely to ash
because in this lifetime you might be winning
but in the next
you   are   next

This is a threat (not a warning) to the fascists

Hark!
You cannot stop me
from deciding to pull the comforter over my head & shield myself
from the morning sun

You cannot stop me
from shedding tears at random places at random times

You cannot stop me
from loving who I love, kissing who I kiss, wanting what I want

You cannot stop me
from hoping for something better for both you & me

You cannot stop me
from fighting for a future worth fighting for

You will not stop a movement stronger than your hate

LA LLAMAN KINGSLAYER

As if it were a bad thing
As if respect means bowing down

When the crown calls their pawns
She says,
I'll show you mine if you show yours first–
talkin' taxes—
because Dear Leader does not pay his

but
la Señora selling elotes sin papeles does—
the one who works
every day
every hour
without PTO
or 401K
or OSHA
or paid breaks
or dull, water cooler conversations on Tuesday afternoons
shivering in first world AC—

She pleads not for a tower with her name
but clean and warm water for her children
and toasty tortillas every morning
with time to make them
hecho de manos limpias
on the garden of her mandil
wiped clean
of laws
of bigots
of Nazis

she tells them
que se vayan a la chingada

then brags to the padre in the confession booth what she told
them racist bastards

it's worth the 10 Ave Marias and 25 Padre Nuestros
just so her knuckles can savor the splintered teeth
she tore off the mad king
like he tore up the constitution of el barrio
the unwritten law that reads

you don't target the most vulnerable

because
when you do,
you pull apart the earth
and when you do
you grant permission to be swallowed whole

parades aren't protests

first Pride was a riot
so, at what point do protests become parades?

bringing out the signs & posters aren't enough
honks by passing spectators aren't enough
clever chants & claps aren't enough

bring out the bricks & post them on windows
stop the spectators in traffic so they can't just pass by
toss the bottles not songs & clap the lighters shut

if there is no disruption there is no point
people gawk at parades
but it is this trouble that leads to change

you're free

It is the dissolution of illusion
that my voice
my choice can be made without permission or consent
undocumented

but

I can still question
the laws
the cops
whoever's in charge
my god
myself
my word
is my bond
that my fists will not unclench
nor my teeth
that will tear through
this leash used to lynch them (not us)
the others are actually us
bending
kneeling
grasping at straws
praying something will save us
from the freedom
they called
they rang
the bells toll
they tell
they shriek
they warn
you're
free
to choose:
salute
or
begone

SIRENS

RED BLUE
RED BLUE
RED BLUE

RED FOR THE WEALTHY
RED FOR THE NAZIS
RED ON THE CLASSROOM WALLS
AGAIN
EVERYTHING RED

BLUE FOR THE MARGINALIZED
BLUE FOR THE CHILDREN
BLUE FROM BEGGING FOR
MORE

EVERYTHING BLUE

RED BLUE
RED BLUE
RED BLUE

BLACK WHITE
SCREECH CLICK
GUN! GUN! GUN! GUN! GUN! GUN!
BANG BANG BANG BANG
BANG BANG
BANG BANG

RED
RED
RED

ONLY EVER RED

IN THE END

Feast

your eyes
on what you have done
choke
on the consequences of your inactions
does it taste salty
or metallic as your response?

devour
while the children pang
while they dream of crumbs
with mouths wide open
and eyes clamped shut

the civilized people
aren't concerned
with the hunger
of others
as long
as their plate
is full

famine is no accident:
it is a crisis built on intentions

the result of
eager incisors
selfish claws
fangs in froth
following the rules
of capitalism
the same ones they put in place

hate the player
AND the game
this shit is rigged
from the Go to the Jail
the winner isn't us
the loser is you
knock the gameboard
dare to be called childish
by the hoarders of wealth

the only rodents
that require an extermination
are the ones calling
for the lives of starving babies

just

it's always
just following orders
just calling the rational alarmists
just flicking the sparks to catch onto gas-
        lighting the past as they burn it down
just rewriting it with bleach
just ensuring it looks about white
just the people being dragged like dead bodies by men who are
just earning scraps & calling it prosperous while 1 percent
just feast on meals baked in the same bread ovens that burned one
                people alive and is starving another

just between me & you
        if it isn't genocide
        why does it
                look
                smell
                feel
                sound
                taste
                bleed
just like it?

Begone

melt

dissolve

evaporate

be gone

disappear
like you made so many

so run
so runny

so run
so running

keep running between these fingers
keep running from these fingers

because if they catch you
when they catch you

I'm afraid
I too will forget how to release

I'm afraid
I too will forget mercy

Shear Faith

I shed (   ) for you

shed as in (blood)
shed as in (tears)
shed as in (skin)

shed as in (whatever)
shed as in (you)
shed as in (want)
for you

I (   ) bled
I (   ) cried
I (   ) tore myself apart

shed as in voluntarily
shed as in happily
shed as in blindly

all for you

for me
do the same—
shed as in suffer
shed as in shrink
shed as in believe
in me
more than
yourself

I know you
won't
for me
(or anyone else)

Winds of change

Are the winds of change supposed to hurt this much?
Are they meant to whisper when it instead whips?
Are whirlwind spirals guiding me in tow or leading me astray?

They leave me sighing
so loud it turns to a howl

I exhaust my lungs
& the disappointment drips
into a pour
into a flood
into tidal waves evaporating
into puddles
dispersing after the
children stomp away
the moisture
leaving only footprints that now turned
to dew for a rising sun to lay pieces of itself on
as the fields recover from the torment
rising as we did when we were born
& laying down only because
we choose to do so

the winds have changed the question from:

Is all we have each other?

to

If all we have are each other, is it true?

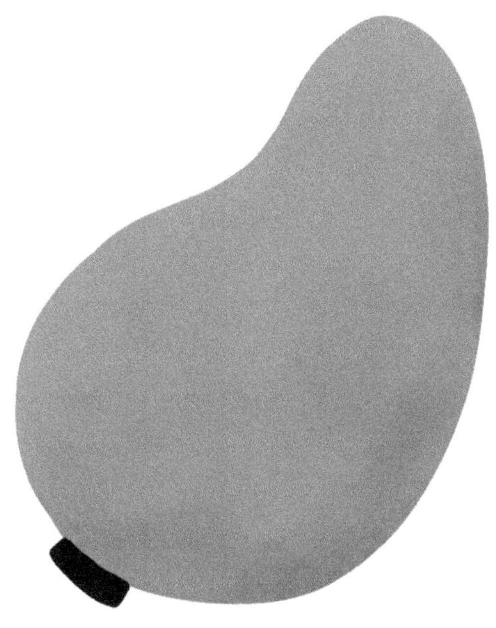

Mango

Sabes quererme

You know how to love me

I want to

feel
the grooves
of
your
body
the way a
needle on a
record player
traces the
lines on
vinyl

read
the
slopes
of your
thighs
the way
blind men
seek
knowledge

fill
t h e g a p s o f y o u r l i p s
w i t h t h e c r a c k s o f m i n e

drown
in the riptides of your eyes
just
to
say
I tried
learning how to swim

be loved

ahogando en agua fresca

If the night were a drink,
it would be this jamaica in our hands

with sweat boiling out,
rolling down
kissing our necks along the way
tenderly leaving sanguine stains pooling
p
u
l
l
i
n
g

drowning
us
in rubicund petals

liquid truth—too honest,
too tart to be lies—
tells us to profess
with summer breath
condensing under a crescent
plunging with us into crimson waves
matching florid eyes
striking the ruddy flesh
like a match scraping the surface
the heat overpours
spilling it all
on our tongues
that thirst, the sparks,
the taste & all

everything's magic

crammed
　　　in a San Francisco studio
sharing
　　　the scene & the hookah mouthpiece

　　　　　　　　　　　　　our breaths undressed

swirling
　　　out of existence together
spinning
　　　like records that made us believe in magic
　　　like our heads from too much consumption
colliding

& our lips

tasting
　　　the rest of our lives

Dropouts (apt 292)

Walmart comforters warm the bodies that adorn the floor along with notebooks & burns from dropping the hookah too many times. A collection of empty rum bottles on display takes up the living room mantle like it was something to be proud of. Twin-size mattresses one-inch-thick separate floor from spines, so when Maria rolls out of bed she does so religiously, like Moses dividing the sea between carpet fibers & Made in China cotton sheets. There is only a green couch with weathered leather resembling moldy, wrinkled skin purchased at the thrift shop for five bucks plus Cristina's tip for the drive. The wall already adorned with a hole behind the poster after Diego & Tomas played baseball indoors with a cardboard tube & bubble wrap Tomas swung & missed the ball but he still got a hit.

On winter's last day,
they ditched class to build a fort
from dollar store sheets

bus stop

it was cold meaning our breaths were no longer secret
our words lingered longer in the air for all to see
our soul escaped momentarily
just to remind you it can swim among stars

& there they were
in line like everyone else
drenched in moonlight

black was their color
it was also mine

they were crowned with long, straight hair so dark
light couldn't escape its grip
or wanted to

I etched to the world
whoa

finding out they were the one

they would open the front door without having to knock
check the fridge when they were hungry
place their shoes next to mine
but it was when they would read a story near the window while I
sat in bed sipping coffee—sharing the static silence—
that I realized it

on the precipice

you & I are

Christmas lights dangling in the middle of July
fireworks lit up before & after the fourth
pumpkins on the porch rotting past November
guayabas jumping to taste the cement of the driveway
nopales flourishing in dirt manifesting soil
sábila with tears donating cures to abuelitas

paper lanterns
on the precipice of annihilation
using destruction to burst brighter than the oblivion
resisting the temptation to burn the mercy we hold

choosing vibrancy   to counter the void

& one another just to

float on

I've Broken Bones for You

So what if I was just a dishwasher?
Or a cook whose English is splintered into pieces?
Or sold roses on the corner of Bristol and 17th?

                Is that embarrassing?

I am just the fingers
that slice fruits
for others I don't know
beneath a rainbow
on a cloudless day
when it should be for you

Would you still love me and show me off?
Even though my knees tremble when I stand
and I smell like crushed camphor 24/7?

                                Is dignity only fit for the wealthy?

So what if my body is all I have to offer?
I make money but it's not enough
Don't you want diamonds and gold?
Food that isn't on sale?
Someone worth showing off—
                worth proclaiming this is who loves me
                                and who I love?

Darling,
I'm just laboring through the days,
blistering through moons that shine brighter than the sun
I can't make enough to keep this house,
and what about us?

Is a roof all you need to have a home?

Fuck money
                                We want love
                                We want us
                                We want more than what we can have

I need not rings

I need not rings
to wrap these fingers
already adorned with yours

nor paper blotted with jargon
from law books
to decree a commitment

made the moment
our eyes locked each other
in a room

tossed the key
fogged the windows
gasped like drinking water for the first time

stopping after turning away
only for us to quench again

lynched at the louvre

I long to be
lynched at the Louvre with you
hanging side-by-side
with the other bodies
of art

Let us decay
side by side
ripped out like teeth leaving only cavities
to be filled
like a depression without a therapy session
like a space between teeth
meant to be fangs,
incisors,
& all
canines piercing only gap
unfulfilled and gapping wide
out

I long to be
lynched at the Louvre with you
with our hurt left on display
our pain to be shared
scoffed
dismissed
entertaining the masses
with our suffering

I long to be
lynched at the Louvre with you
where we can be statues
sculpted out of earth
left in the kiln a bit too long
hardened into fabric velvet draped
bleeding like pastel left dangling

put us on display
in the center
open us up like an autopsy
like cadavers worth violating

I long to be
lynched at the Louvre with you
worthy of showing the wounds
so our abusers
our prosecutors
the wielders of weapons like words
whose prayers of theirs
whipped and peeled off
the layers of flesh
may discover that degloved, darker
flesh is still colored like flesh
no matter the mutilation

May I long be with you
stolen
unforgiven
never forgotten

May the framing of our sorrow glisten with gold
until it's okay

the infliction of pain is okay
as long as
it is able to be sold & packaged
into brands & logos
into status symbols
showing that while we are in disarray
at least others can dangle
their agony & arrogance

So
let's hang
together maybe
down the back, but
who cares—
it's still the louvre

Family Album: Mi papá

This is my father
mi papá
He wields that same smile—the one that always stretched a
moustache to his cheeks
erupting the dimples concealed beneath
a canopy of overgrown stubble flourishing machismo

the same smile I'd look forward to after showing him something
new
the same smile I have seen
but not felt since then

He is not the center of this photo
But is no doubt the subject
the only person facing the lens
the main character
the cook not chef
the underdog who's paid under the table
the model of manhood for his sons
&
the mistakes of following him

He dawns a white button-up & apron appearing almost holy
only missing the glow of a halo
yet he's still Saint Grill Boy

His eyes meet the photographer's
even though they share not rings
they do children
they do homes
they do sins
pupils latch like the attachment of an addict
one who loves hard & hurts harder
a seeker of something to expunge the agony

He chooses her at the moment so strongly the film captures it
the grip is so tight it creases the corners
to the center where the grill exhales smoke

smudging the frame of what was evident back then as it is now
he looks at Mami in a way that says
this is all worth it to go home to you

&
I choose to remember him this way
when I still called him Papi & he called me mijo

Family Album: Mami

This is my mother
mi mamá
    smiling so wide her teeth are showing, which she never allows
        claims the metal crowns aren't worth showing

    holding my hand as we walk down the steps
    with papeles long-sought declaring her legalized
        in a language that jammed itself between her jaws
        unhinging the joints until the acentos are sawed off
        so the tongue can no longer roll
            but she can still roll masa
            like she rolls with the punches
            like she rolls & swirls when she dances to La Chona
            like her last bead of sweat rolling onto the
                dancefloor
            like she rolls out of bed en la madrugada the
                day after
            like my eyes roll when she tries to speak to me in
                this unhinged tongue

she looks across to me
    waiving a flag of some place called home
    me oblivious
        to the hours of Inglés sin Barreras
        she studied with her sisters
        or the hours of overtime
        spent elbows deep in chemicals,
        scouring dried ketchup from tables,
        withstanding searing oil hurdling from the fryer
        to the point the cartilage of the knees will wane
        & no number of massages from abuelita will help

& it still won't be enough
enough money
American enough
Good enough

but for me,
it's more than enough

Below the (poverty) line

They tried their best to
hide it, but the clues were
there to be picked up anytime
they were accidently dropped.

It was the cans. Picked out of
the public trash bins stomped
as Amá made it into a game of
crushing the best aluminum circle.

It was the constant arroz y frijoles
con tortillas served morning &
evening that somehow never lost
its flavor to the consistency.

It was the number of channels
on the TV, but as long as the
antennae—clad in the same
foil used for topping the ollas—
was at the right angle to iron
out the static, it would reveal
channel 11 in time for the Simpsons.

It was riding the bus. Preschool
in the mornings with mami
whose hair was done immaculately
& exuded the scent of Suave
shampoo & clothes baptized in
Zote. Then to work in the afternoons
to the Madona's or Greel Boy, to
home smelling like Happy Meals
& sweat undoing all the effort.

It was the house. My own bed
was in the living room, folded
& rolled to the corner during
the day. The wall shared three
extra rooms built without

the city's permission & a trailer
that would rust alongside
the lime tree in the backyard.

It was the trees. Proving how
many living beings could
flourish on that minute corner
property. We were blessed with
aguacates, guayabas, limones,
sábila, nopales, chicharros,
huajes, botellas de Bud Light,
tiles papi swore he'd use to
re-do the kitchen, soda mami
complained was bad for us but
we still had because it was part
of the deal at Northgate, & food.
Lots of food.

& people. It was the people.
The house was fed people &
it never starved. Growing
abundant like our bellies would.
It was where everyone threw
parties. I would proudly host
my primos to the jumper suffocating
the patchy grass. The kids would
switch the motor on & off as
they escaped the collapsing
palace, trying to outrun the tidal
wave of rubber, crashing into each
other to escape if the motor wasn't
turned back on in time. This was
our fun. We would stumble back
to the always white folding chairs
& tables rented for the weekend
dressed in dollar store covers held
by 99-cent tape, topped with clear
plastic napkin holders recycled for the
event to be inevitably hosted next month.
Papis would crowd the cooler or
the grill or hold on to the brick wall

for balance after tipping over
their fifth tinted glass bottle lined
up on the cement like a child who
only knows one way to play with
dominoes.

Mamis would be caressed by the
squealing folding chairs, huddling
to share chisme like the chalice
that held prophet blood at misa
where all would sip & pass along
the holy spirit.

How could I have known when I
had all these riches? Only to be
told that was actually called *poverty*.

Sábila

Sacando espinas

Extracting the spines

me dijeron

entré en este mundo lleno de palabras
que aprendí de los mismos antepasados
que me instruyeron a hablar cuando estaba listo
así que grité con mis pulmones al mundo
hasta que entré en el aula
donde enjaularon mi boca

ataron una soga y me dijeron que la envolviera alrededor
de mi lengua
dijeron que era por mi propio bien
como si fuera sólo una nalgada
como si esto no fuera un linchamiento
como si me lo merecía por ser quien era
se sentía familiar mientras miraba a su armadura brillante
e inhalaba su viruela

me dijeron que despojara mi lenguaje
sólo para que me dijeran que usara su propia marca de la misma
como si lo recogieron del mercado de pulgas
con la costura todo torcido y la tilde faltando
el logotipo es al revés y la etiqueta dice *Made in the USA*
pero sé que fue robado de otro lugar

me alimentaron con queso del gobierno
y me regurgitaron su idioma
llamaron a mi tortilla con arroz y frijoles insalubre
mientras bebían en su *large Coke*

con el tiempo aprendí a amar el almuerzo en la escuela
así como aprendí a odiar mi propio acento
y me olvidé como rodar masa y la letra R

hasta mis padres creían en esta extraña religión
donde confesamos nuestro pecado de hablar español
de nacer con piel manchada como lodo
con ojos el color de suelo estéril
y empecé a blanquear mi discurso
porque mi piel era demasiado oscura

odiaba a quien una vez amaba
y lo hice de nuevo una vez que comencé a amar a quien soy

porque me di cuenta que olvidé cómo decir *I'm sorry* en español
como las plantas junto a mi ventana, mi español era falso

nunca creció ni tenia oportunidad a empezar crecer
sólo parecía vivo porque al menos si fuera real volvería a crecer
así que voy a empezar de nuevo con tierra fresca
y lo regaré hasta que aprendo cómo decir *te perdono*

ahora estoy tratando de llenarme con las mismas palabras que nací
con que me derramé en el camino
ahora entiendo que estoy dotado de piel el color del suelo
de crecimiento y de la resiliencia
no seré domesticado por la vergüenza porque yo soy orgulloso
yo soy lo que hicieron mis antepasados
lo mismos que me instruyeron a hablar cuando estaba listo

estoy listo

I was told

I entered this world full of words
that I learned from the same ancestors
who instructed me to speak when I was ready
so, I screamed with my lungs to the world
until I entered the classroom
where they caged my mouth

they handed me a rope & told me to wrap it around my tongue
they said it was for my own good
as if it was just a spanking
as if this wasn't a lynching
as if I deserved it for being who I was
it felt familiar as I looked at their shining armor & inhaled their smallpox

they told me to strip my language
only to be told to use their own brand of it
like they picked it up at a flea market
with the stitching all twisted & the tilde missing
the logo upside down & the tag decrees *Made in the USA*
but I know it was stolen from somewhere else

they fed me government cheese & regurgitated their language to me
called my tortilla con arroz y frijoles unhealthy
while they sipped on their large Coke
over time, I learned to love school lunch
just as I learned to hate my own accent
& I forgot how to roll masa & the letter R

even my parents believed in this strange religion
where we confessed our sin of speaking Spanish
of being born with soiled skin & barren soil-colored eyes
& I started to bleach my speech because my skin was too dark
I hated who I once loved
& I did it again once I started to love who I am

because I realized I forgot how to say *I'm sorry* in Spanish
like the plants by my window, my Spanish was fake
it never grew nor had a chance to start growing

it only seemed alive because at least if it were real,
it would grow again

so, I'll start over with fresh soil
& I'll water it until I learn how to say *I forgive you*
now I'm trying to fill myself with the same words I was born with
that I spilled along the way
now I understand that I am gifted with skin the color of earth, of
growth, of resilience
I will not be domesticated by shame because I am proud, I am what
my ancestors made me
the same ones who instructed me to speak when I was ready

I am ready

reattach

lop off pieces of yourself to fit into their mold
what a strange shape you become
done something that can't be undone
unwell is that others have shoved their beliefs
onto an infant not older than two, three breaths
they search & zoom onto a part they claim is private
saying this is for your own good & we have to
save
          it
                    into a her
                    or he
                        (somebody worth saving)

the binary is reinforced
the status quo safe & sound
from your difference
your body is a battleground—
slurs and bullets hurled throughout,
still, you raise your flag stating you're still there—
          god
                    damn
                              right
you're still there
& breathing
& alive
& trying your best to thrive

you can only bury a body so deep
until it becomes part of the trees
roots planted & it starts with a heave
in & out
into the world so proudly proclaimed

proclaim
pick up the pieces
& attach them back
to a natural piece of the earth

Leaving ≠ Healing

I
Defund SAPD

Amtrak shakes the house
Bodies are outlined in chalk
Caution tape outside
Helicopters & sirens
Tell me: "Stay safe—stay away"

II
I hope she stopped

Even when she smiled,
I thought of her thighs & the
last time I felt them
Her bronze skin thawed my fingers
when I traced the copper scars

III
After moving to the Bay Area at 18

I promised not to
dye my hair or get tattoos
So, when I returned
with blue strands & a pierced lip,
Mom asked where the tattoo was.

Home

is a table
topped with tortillas
surrounded by brown faces
who have carried me once

a father, proud of his son
a mother, relieved
a sister, enthused
a brother, well-intended

These people
round a square table
The main attraction plays along
boasting he never missed them too much

He did

Tiger Stripes

I earned them when I was 11
I first noticed them in the bathroom mirror as I was
unfurling layers of clothing before setting foot in the shower

Fissures climbed my shoulders & faults crowded my belly
They only dug deeper & stretched out as the tremors of time passed by

The shades of brown engulfing my torso wavered
I inherited skin the color of Zihuatanejo white sand to eroded Guanajuato soil
It was the uneven colors on my skin that irked me most
or the idea that even if I didn't work in the fields, this tan owned me
No nopal needed in el frente because the borders wrapped my arms, thighs, & nape

An imposter from birth: pocho or illegal
either
neither
both

Deported to somewhere between
        Mexican appeasement & American appetite
        between shame & pride
        arroz y frijoles & rice & beans

Brown doesn't embrace my entire self
But yo sabo enough to enrage los güeros
Pero not enough to satisfy the gente

Despite trying to scrub off the stains all over my skin
bathing in buckets of bleach
using pomadas probably holding lead
& believing my skin was damaged
I am still all parts
either
neither
both

I learned, maybe too late, that the human body echoes growth
This body adorned with perfect imperfections
is bursting at the seams
cracking throughout
& pulling apart the earth that is the skin
remaining eager to boast what lies below the surface
& beyond all boarders

remember

remember
kneeling before them
how they would wield their weapons of mass destruction
as if they wouldn't one day lead to the annihilation of all

remember
their voices spewing something poison
proclaiming something sacred
holy hands trying to navigate the holy waters of its owners' body
up

down
left right

remember
how they acted as if they weren't the ones lost
with shining armor eclipsing their heart
blinding all along their way

remember
hair was only hewed when death arrived
which explains why they cut ours as soon as they appeared
as if they knew what they were doing

remember
it's easy to tower over someone that was forced to kneel

THERE ARE NO WRONG DECADES ONLY THOSE DOING THE WRONGING

Land of opportunity
is actually
land of chance
to be born
in the wrong decade
one where you're
gassed up in gasoline baths
or
encaged by Juan Crow
or
operated by Operation Wetback
or
stripped of your Zoot Suits
or

one
where you are detained
when you should feel enraged
you are free to speak
just not ill against their president
their idol
their dictator

Dear leader,
I fear
no king
no God
especially if you is all you got

Send your army wielding untouchable and invincible
it's happening again
the armor is just a little bit different
the name isn't Cortez
but the blood runs imperialism

Conquest means kidnapping
ICE means melt
Resist means rise
Protest means people
I mean us
I mean we
I mean we deserve

respect

so do

the Papi's in neon long sleeves enduring sunshine every day to sow beautiful pastures that once yielded fields of fruit

so do

the Mami's bussing it in pristine uniforms to El Toro, Northgate, El Super, but she is the real Superior one

so do

Las señoras—hood abuelitas—limping with reusable bags not meant to be reused carrying plastic bottles to be recycled for income condensed into cubes fit into pockets pinched for misa, for masa, por más un poco más

so do

Los señores—hood abuelitos—pushing raspados o mangos o nieve or ringing sweet sounds of summer echoing, beckoning, inviting all to gather over glistening joy to marvel how we made it this far

so do

Los niños, nuestros niños, robbing their tongue now their loved ones
When will it ever be enough?
When their use is gone, they are called anchors doomed to drown after being thrown overboard

so do

Our hermanos y hermanas trans
our siblings who have suffered inside and outside of the family

let us make sure home is where they are welcome
to take up space
to be safe
to be loved

I digress
this isn't progress
this is regress
this isn't a mistake
this is their play
remember the U.S. modeled what Nazis would do
it's only returning the favor

Por favor
No more
Let this night lower its knives
Let this match light the new day
Let this brick guide my throw
Let us
keep us safe

NoThing is ever lost

I know

Not everyone has vanished
to ash sifting in the Santa Ana winds
nor desiccated under the drought of a thousand summers

Not all were buried alive
to be drowned under pavement–permanent caskets
stepped on for progress they say

NoThing is ever lost
it is only ever given or taken
each day feels closer to the latter

I don't know

What lies in their light but it
flashes, sparkles, beams,
backs me into the corner

What must be done to make it undone won't be
but hope stands
even if I do not

WhatEver will be
& even if they don't allow me to

I know

I will remain

To those like us,

This is not a punishment for being ourselves,
but a reminder that the fight to be is never-ending.
our existence is an act of resistance,
so live

Each inhale unwinds what has kept us chained—
a gravity reflecting the situation that weighs down on a chest
that's always cracking but
refusing to cave in

Each exhale loosens the grip that oppression has on the neck, releasing, ever so minutely, from what has fed this deliberate cycle often mistaken for misfortune & disguised as destiny

Continue to stay despite the alure to run or escape
continue speaking up for those whose tongues have been severed
continue to
continue

This is yet another struggle—
one of many before & of more to appear—
allow even the pettiness to fuel your presence

Live

out of spite, if anything
to savor the joy still abundant in this world
to wield the smiles & wrinkles you deserve

The mourning after

Hurt
is who I am most familiar with
no knocks nor search warrant needed
because like ICE it will also infringe when not invited
especially when uninvited

it is loyal & will stalk from afar
as you spend time laughing with loved ones so it can remind you
that

it is an anchor heavier than those of enslaver ships
heaved across the Atlantic
slitting scars onto the soil that would be proclaimed the land of the free

it is the tears of my students who are growing familiar with Hurt
while asking me what happens
now that the bad guys won?

it is me responding that the villains cannot triumph as long there is

Hope
is the salt on my wound that mixes with Hurt to become

Disappointment
is the literal red flags that were brandished like a gun aimed at our autonomy
it is knowing loss was a possibility but settling on joy to wave right back
it is the fact that they did not miss the bullseye on our backs
it is what you tell yourself as you always have:
this is why you always keep your head & voice down
this is why you must avoid the clutches of optimism like the plague it is
this is why you don't invest your entire self, lest you walk away bankrupt
this is why you shouldn't try pursuing your own vision of

Redemption
is over the horizon / behind the moon / under the couch
but it is not lost forever

Hereditary

I was the last to find out that abuelita died
I felt a tug on one of my heartstrings
it wasn't a pull, though, like when the last of my abuelitos passed
I didn't even know her name
she was just abuelita & phone calls
full of false promises of returning to Mexico to see her

I think I related more to Apá's father
because he hung himself
 because that was when I found out
 self-destruction is hereditary

It makes sense now
that night I almost beat him to the grave
why for the longest time I sought relief from a buried ache—
 I was born with a wick to my brain—
 surviving despite being surrounded by cinders

Apá didn't have a chance
 because they don't teach you psychology in la primaria
 when school stopped at 4th grade
 you graduated to working with your hands
 accepting the tingling in the fingers
 swallowing the burning swelling around the spine
 ignoring potential for what is probably forever

 his wick tethered to the liver clasping to a bottle of
 Tecate, Corona, Pacifico, Modelo, Bud Light…
 addiction can be beautiful if you look at the remains—
 shards of glass reflecting cityscape lights on body outlines

Amá also didn't have a chance
 because only two sexes existed & one had to labor more
 through their body—bending, twisting, splitting, spreading
 enough to splinter but not break—
 growing afraid of abandonment
 to the point of mistaking manipulation for love
 porque niñas buenas se quedan calladitas depending on a
 man to be her savior

leading to marrying her abuser
her wick ran to her heart, sprinting throughout the arteries
radiating in pulses present on palms flicking coal-hot tortillas
digits coated in callouses and a ring rusting like wrinkles
she loved hard, almost too hard, becoming someone to be
taken advantage of

Especially my brother who had no chance
a first-born raised by chanceless cycles turning and churning
another one
baptized in bigotry
drowning in patriarchy
fluent in homophobia
victim of a victim taking another victim
whose wick was a cry for attention that was blamed on
Gangs
Satan
TV
video games
junk food
boredom
anything but the actual system
that buries mental health
covers it with dirt
and when it's unearthed
it is blamed on
Gangs
Satan
TV
video games
junk food
boredom
anything but the actual system

I stopped wanting to be saved at an early age
I posited that god didn't care if I ate carne on Fridays during Lent
or if I preferred men
or if I didn't attend church
or if I adorned my skin in permanent art

my wick is buffering dynamite ready to implode
delicate like love handles waiting to be held

thirsty hands calling out for water drying out in Santa Ana sun
though my wick is ready to be lit
fire can be smothered as easy as it is sparked

Mami would joke

as we collected so many beer cans from our backyard
that we could build a home made out of them

I stopped laughing when I realized this house already existed
& we lived in it

at that moment, though, I promised

te construiré un hogar de oro
no aluminio aplastado para caber en las bolsas de basura

con agua limpia
y arboles llena de frutas
y nopales sin espinas
y huajes para los vecinos
y guayabas que nunca se pudren encima de los carros
y el aguacate todavía creciendo donde papi lo quemó

el mismo donde soñé de mi propia casita
encima de las mismas ramas donde podía
ver la familia de tlacuaches escondiendo de papi
armado con su botella y pistola
una lanzando vidrio y otro quebrando su propia familia
y después culpándolos por lo que hizo con sus propias manos
los mismos que antes nos tocó tan tiernamente prometiendo al
mundo
hasta que dejó de creerlo

but I promise Mami again
this won't stay like this forever

On the car stereo a corrido about us plays

a brass heartbeat tenderly rocks
the reflections in the rearview mirror
like papi cradling us in his big, brown arms
& my big, brown cheeks surrendering
to the hairy sleeves

the accordion sings
the color bright yellow
drips mango
& drizzles cempasúchil petals

the bajo quinto strums
with a metallic twang
hoisting the melody
with all five pairs of steel hands

through the speakers

the singer
recounts
the time mami cried when she told her mami she was
choosing coyote over femicide

the singer
describes a boy in Guanajuato who followed the green
light only to become Grill Boy

the singer
tells the story of when Grill Boy met girl
working in a Sizzler in Reagan's America
& how their fingers interlocked
even as the world tried to ply them apart

we sing along to the chorus
of us,

tracing the notes
as if they were grains of sand
as if it was number one in the charts
as if we didn't know how the song ends

still
we smile along

because who else
was this song
written for
but us?

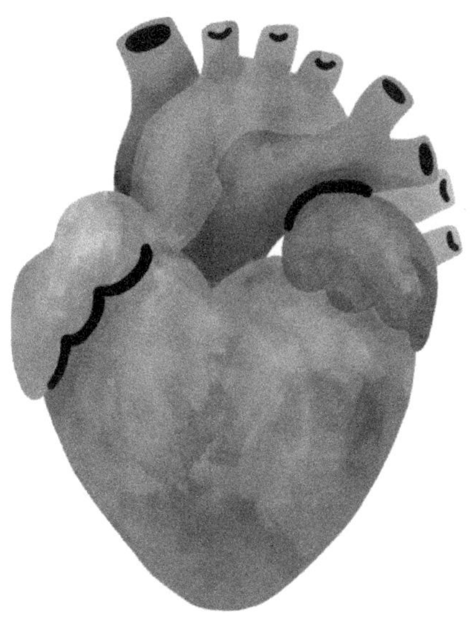

ACKNOWLEDGMENTS

I greatly appreciate the editors of the following literary presses where earlier versions of these poems first appeared in some shape or form:

826LA

Alegría Publishing

Angel City Review

Black Fox Literary Magazine

Community Milk

Daxson Publishing

FlowerSong Press

Gnashing Teeth Publishing

Loud Coffee Press

Moon Tide Press

MUSE

¡Pa'lante!

Pluto's Zine

Polemical Zine

San Diego Poetry Annual

The Ear

The ILL Anthology (Curious Publishing)

Xinachtli Journal (Journal X)

THANK YOU

First, and always first, thank you to my partner, my best friend, my love, Hannah. You are a partner in every sense of the word. Someone I share and part my life with. That includes every aspect of this book from the title to the poems to the layout, the author photo, and so much more than anyone else can think of. My editor, photographer, designer, and source of happiness, thank you. This, or anything else positive in my life, is indebted to you. I look forward to many more projects and adventures we have planned for in the future. Thank you. Thank you. A billion times over, thank you.

This body of work is built on the words of everyone I encountered, read, watched, and heard. This includes a plethora of iconic names like Rudy Francisco, Andrea Gibson, Melissa Lozada-Oliva, Sabrina Benaim, Yesika Salgado, Karla Cordero, and Natalie Diaz just to name a few. Along with poet laureates, past and present, who I met and inspire me including Gustavo Hernandez, Camille Hernandez, Ceasar K. Avelar, and Natalie Sierra who ensure their words and wisdom are accessible to the communities they serve.

Thank you to my peers and contemporaries who secure safe spaces so that our voices are heard and foster one another to become better writers and people: Sofía Aguilar, Anatalia Vallez, Jesus Cortez, Sarah Rafael García, Lizeth De La Luz, Allie Rigby, Sam Robertson, Lizzette Barrios Gracián, Joe Rosati, Satnam Narang, Celeste Alyssa Gomez, Sammy/Lola, Peter Lechuga, Alejandra J. Lopez, Oscar Velazquez, Summertime Jazz, Wes Blake The Misfit Poet, Redemption the Poet, M.K. Sullivan, J. Saravia, Juan Amador, Maestro DeSean, Tomi Simmons, Paula Macena, Erica Castro and more. So many more. I apologize if I did not name you. I promise you mean the world to me.

Thank you to my family. Especially mi mamá and hermana.

Thank you to the city of Santa Ana, you are forever my home no matter what. Also, to the people who reside under the water tower, relish a raspado, sniff the flowers from the vendors on intersections, and scatter seeds of joy and resistance throughout your city.

ABOUT THE AUTHOR

Alexis Jaimes is a poet and educator from Santa Ana, California. As the proud son of Mexican immigrants, his work explores the intersections of cultural memory, language, generational trauma, and healing. He is the author of the chapbook *Corazón Coalesced* published through Bottlecap Press. His work has appeared in numerous presses as well as showcased at the Fullerton Museum Center and the Huntington Beach Art Center. When he's not writing, he teaches in a dual-language classroom, believing in the power of language in all its forms. Alexis can also be found hosting or attending open mics throughout Orange County.

Contact Alexis at:

letrasbyalex@gmail.com
letrasbyalex.com
@letrasbyalex on Instagram

PUBLISHER'S NOTE

Daxson Publishing was created to help marginalized artists and their allies publish their work, so the world can hear their voice. The vision for this publishing house is to help people get their work out there, and not have them struggle finding their way through the publishing process. Everyone's voice deserves to be heard, and we are here to help. If you are interested in submitting a manuscript, email daxsonpublishing@gmail.com. Support our cause! Buy our books at daxsonpublishing.com.

AUTHOR'S NOTE

Per the publisher's request, it must be noted that this book intentionally does not follow typical printing standards. From the spread for the table of contents to the seperation between sections, these blank pages serve as seperators as well as spaces to breathe amongst the topics covered in the book. It is the author's hope that this serves to enhance the reader's experience and the narrative as a whole. Thank you.

www.ingramcontent.com/pod-product-compliance
Ingram Content Group UK Ltd.
Pitfield, Milton Keynes, MK11 3LW, UK
UKHW062305290726
14090UKWH00018B/898

9 781966 337416